Home Study Edition

The

Wooden Dummy

Our

Forgiving Friend

Copyright Mark Beardsell 2016

Index

Chapter	Page
Dedication	3
Preface	4
History of the Dummy	5
My Journey	6
Section One - Form - Side One	10
Section One - Form - Side Two	17
Section Two - Form - Performed once	24
Section Two - Form - Side One	27
Section Two - Form - Side Two	29
Section Three - Form - Performed Once	32
Section Three - Form - Side One	34
Section Three - Form - Side Two	36
Section Four - Po Pie Chueng	40
Section Four - Form - Performed Once	40
Section Four - Form - Application One	41
Section Four - Form - Left Side Strike	42
Section Four - Form - Back to Centre	43
Section Four - Form - Right Side Strike	45
Section Five - Form	47
Section Six – Form	52
Section Seven - Form	58
Dummy Application	65
Common types of dummy	86
The Full form	89
Thanks	120

Dedication:

First and foremost, this book is dedicated to all of those past and present who have guided me on my Wing Chun journey who continue to inspire me, and without whose knowledge, guidance and patience it would not have been possible to pass on this gift to help those on similar paths achieve their goals- this book embodies my gratitude.

A big thanks to my late father for his insatiable thirst for knowledge of martial arts and for dragging me to classes without which I would not have been able to write this book or to have lived this life.

I would also like to thank my teacher and friend Grandmaster Samuel Kwok for taking me under his wing and for passing on the Wing Chun of Ip Man in accordance with his wishes so that it will not be forgotten, which I, in turn will pass on to as many people as I can so that it will spread and thrive in all seasons like branches stemming from a great tree nourishing the global martial arts community with its apple of wisdom.

Preface

The dummy form or wooden man form which is pronounced in Cantonese as 'mook yan chong', is mostly taught after the biu jee form, however you can learn it after chum kiu depending on who your teacher is, just make sure that you do not train beyond what you have learned. It is better to have a few strengths than many weaknesses.

With that being said, if you are a person who has nobody to train Wing Chun with then the wooden dummy can be your forgiving friend- however you should not train the actual form; you should practice the techniques that you have learned up to now on the dummy. You also may consider looking for a cheap second hand one as dummies tend to cost a lot of money and after all a second hand one in mint condition is no different to a fresh dummy barring a hopefully considerably reduced price.

There are varieties in the arm positioning of dummies due to different construction techniques but this is purely due to the mechanics of the individual carpentry and should not affect your martial arts progress. It is important that your dummy has a leg as you also need to practice your footwork. There are cheaper half dummies and flat ones but whilst they are cheaper they will not offer always the correct angling and recoil and so it can be false economy i.e. money saved now but perfection of fighting form tainted later.

The dummy is a tool to partially replace a live opponent however it is not a full substitute but merely a vital part of the progression of your Wing Chun training. I should also point out that this book uses Cantonese terminology and explanations which in part relies on the reader having a previous understanding of the fundamentals of Wing Chun.

History of the dummy

In my research in to the origins of the wooden dummy, I found a story that stems from the Shaolin temple, for those that watched the TV series Kung Fu starring the late David Carradine you will remember that in order for him to leave the temple he had to go through a right of passage ending with the lifting of a hot cauldron with symbols on the side to another pressure pad to open the door, thus burning the symbols into his arms like branding. With this in mind it was said that one such right of passage to leave the temple was to complete a challenge in a room with 108 wooden dummies of all types and on completion they could following the cauldron trial leave the temple. Of course there is no way to prove the accuracy of the story and it could be an anecdotal teaching aid but many tall tales are trees with a seed of truth at the core.

The Wing Chun dummy as you know has 108 or 116 movements in depending on how you end each section of the form. The original dummies used in Wing Chun were buried into the ground and sometimes wooden arms and legs may have been built into a tree with suitable flexibility and in the most basic or desperate of occasions the tree utilised unaltered in its natural form. There came a time when Ip Man finally became recognised for his skills based on the fame of Lee Jun Fan (Bruce Lee) by this time Ip Man was living in Hong Kong and ground space was very limited and in the early days Ip Man did not have a dummy so he taught his students the form in the air, there came a time for Ip Man when this became a problem so he approached a carpenter by the name of Fung Shek and they devised a way of mounting a dummy on the wall of an upstairs apartment and so the wall mounted dummy was born.

My Journey

My personal journey was no different to anyone else's, after messing around with various martial arts over a lot of years, I learned a lot but I never dedicated myself to just one. I and my father went off to Judo, Aikido and Karate classes quite religiously like clockwork. One day I finally decided that I was going to focus solely on one martial art and to master it, but which one? I had no clue, so having the internet at my disposal I started to look around, joining martial arts bulletin boards and firing off emails to anyone who could provide some shred of wisdom or iota enthusiasm.

My prior history with assorted martial arts gave me some insight into what to look for in terms of effectiveness and legitimacy. I looked at various Kung Fu styles and tried to really get in to Aikido but I was really struggling with the Japanese language aspect that was so integral to it. I finally found Jeet Kune Do and took a look at it via a DVD and spotted another style in the DVD called Wing Chun, having a trained eye I could see there was lot that I could learn from this art, and started looking for a local school.

Unfortunately, I could not find a group in my region, but I was not going to give up, I looked for the closest schools to me and evaluated the logistics of getting there and back within the same evening.

As I examined the art more closely I started to utilise the internet's market places to buy up and absorb any aids and literature that might be of help to my Wing Chun development- even within the most dubious of materials like finding a lotus blossom in a mangrove swamp a pearl of wisdom might be found amidst both the mumbo jumbo and the legitimate heritage of the art.

Being brand new to the art I started dropping emails to the prominent masters in my area- being an unfamiliar novice many emails met with a less than enthusing response if any reaction at all however this did not dent my thirst for progress. I spent a lot of time reading articles about the art, and I found movies and training videos and watched everything I could trawling sites like YouTube to discover Wing Chun in all of its myriad of varied forms. As I studied the videos and it became apparent that the majority of people were doing a similar version but there were people (masters) who were doing it differently, this helped guide me towards the common schools and lineages. I finally focused in on Ip Man's Wing Chun, I just needed to find someone who could teach me it...

I then considered distance learning as a final option, and explored several online options some of which were a little unsatisfactory, then I found one in Arizona that had a proper structured grading system and curriculum. It may not have been a perfect fit but it was helpful and my enthusiasm kicked in. The combination and culmination of video lessons, recording myself for feedback and eagerly leafing through books promoted by the course fuelled and fed my growing knowledge of Wing Chun but reached the point where the next stage would require human interaction on a real time and spontaneous level...such was my zeal that I flew from the United Kingdom to Chicago on a Friday, trained the next day and flew right back across the Atlantic Ocean to England on the Sunday. The novelty was dizzying and did much to not only inspire me to discover more but also to offset the exhaustion induced by that rigorous travel. The next year I visited Arizona, and was absolutely blown away with what I had found there plus the rigorous exercise and travel caused me to quit my twenty plus daily cigarette habit which alone markedly improved my quality of life...this was another health benefit that really blossomed with my complete immersion into the martial arts community.

After several years with the same organisation, I was alerted to a week-long Wing Chun camp located in Portugal and feeling somewhat brash I attended the camp and actually adopted this variation of Wing Chun following many comprehensive conversations with my apartment mate long into the night. This switch in schools was simply a result of what felt instinctively right to me and was regardless of the fame or fortune of the various masters on the circuit.

Now at his point I was still training with my first school and learning what my new schools were doing and so I became multifaceted in the art of Wing Chun.

I was still looking at what other people were doing and spotted an online course whereby you could test for the first two forms Siu Lim Tau and Chum Kiu and then test for the Dummy form called Mook Yan Jong, most schools made you do all of the empty hand forms first, so I took the opportunity to get in there and do it.

Eventually I discarded the first course as it proved too different from what the second and third course were doing, and continued to travel the world from deepest Asia to Western Europe and the Americas.

While all this was going on, whilst I was looking for local people to train with I ended up forming a local Wing Chun School, which had always seemed more a dream of the future than an actual achievable physical reality yet here it was.

So after travelling world and meeting a multitude of new people and making a lot of new friends I have become a prominent martial artist known worldwide, I have my own successful distance learning product and have students throughout the globe, I have written 5 books and created a DVD series, and the journey is just beginning with no end in sight.

Section One - Form - Side One

When you approach the dummy to set yourself up in front of it, stand to attention, then put both of your hands at full extension on the dummy's body horizontal to the ground, then step forward slightly, now drop your hands in to the fighting guard called bai chong, this is achieved by opening your stance with hoi ma then putting your left hand out into man sau then your right hand should be in wu sau.

Left man sau

The first move of the form is achieved by bending your knees, and then springing back up and making contact with your left man sau, we now have a bridge point to the dummy which means that if you don't use your eyes and only listen with your wrist through the form you will develop a better understanding of how to utilise recoil and energy, however until you have learned it don't try it blind folded- accidents will happen and confidence needs to equal practiced ability first.

Right Juk cheung / Left lap sau

Switching positions, using the hand that was in man sau grab (lap sau) the wooden arm it is touching then the hand that was in wu sau shoot that hand forward into the wooden dummied head area that could be imagined as the neck area of a human.

Right Man geng sau

From here reach the hand that struck the neck around the back of the dummy's head area you may notice its hard to reach, that's because you should turn the body into a sideling stance with your feet and waist at 45 degrees, and from there, with a short jerk from the waist (yiu ma) pull the neck hand and the lap sau hand simultaneously.

Right Bong sau

Using the sideling stance you can easily drop the hand that is currently located around the back of the neck to bong sau on the inside of the dummy's right arm- it's on your left.

Tan da

Maintaining contact with your bong sau, and stepping to the left side, your bong sau hand should roll nicely into tan sau, circle your right leg behind the dummy's leg on the side you are standing and dai cheung your left hand into the dummy's area between the two upper arms and the lower arms, but make all these move in one flowing unhesitant action- this is how the power is released. Any needless delay will needlessly diffuse and dilute the power that you unleash so the onus is acting as one and instantly coordinating into a single action.

High Jum/low gaan

Rotating your leg out from behind the dummy's leg and place it down into a 45 degree sideling stance facing right as you do so use the left hand that is currently in dai cheung to form a jum sau on the outside of the right dummy arm, at the same time your hand that is in tan sau to gaan sau and makes contact with the lower single arm.

Kwun sau

With a half step, move to the right and switch hands so that the gaan sau on the lower single arm comes up and hits the inside of the dummy's left arm and the hand currently in a high jum sau should drop down and make contact with the right side of the lower single arm, this should all happen simultaneously this action is called kwun sau, rotating hands.

Disconnected Tan da

Disconnecting your arms from the dummy step right a little further than you did when you went to the left, having your left man sau up and your right wu sau launch forward locking out the dummy leg with your left leg, block the dummy left arm on the outside using tan sau and hit the dummy chest area with dai cheung and again I reiterate for emphasis this should all happen simultaneously.

The Wooden Dummy – Our Forgiving friend

High Jum/low gaan

Rotating your leg out from behind the dummy's leg and place it down into a 45 degree sideling stance facing left as you do so use the right hand that's is currently in dai cheung to form a jum sau on the outside of the left dummy arm, at the same time your hand that is in tan sau to gaan sau and makes contact with the lower single arm.

Left high jum/right heun sau

Coming to the end of the first part of the form circle your right hand over the dummy's left arm so your hand ends up blocking the inside of that arm, then bringing your arm that is currently in gaan sau in a slight curve to the outside of the dummy's right arm into an upper pointing jum sau so you should be looking at the palm of the left hand with fingers pointing upwards

Left lap sau / right jing cheung

Take your left hand currently in jum sau and grab that arm you are currently connected to and hit the dummy with palm up of the right hand slamming it into the dummy's face area. and finish in bai chong ready for the next section unless you like to finish with a double jum sau and a double tok sau.

Section One - Form - Side Two

Right Kiu Sau

Because your right hand is currently in wu sau, you need to change guard hands to make the bridge point so again you should bounce on the knees just like you did when starting the form.

Left Juk Cheung / Right lap Sau

Switching positions, using the hand that was in man sau grab (lap sau) the wooden arm it is touching then the hand that was in wu sau shoot that hand forward into the wooden dummied head area that could be imagined as the neck area of a person.

Left Man Geng Sau

From here reach the hand that struck the neck around the back of the dummy's head area- you may notice its hard to reach, that's because you should turn the body into a sideling stance with your feet and waist at 45 degrees, and from there, with a short jerk from the waist (yiu ma) pull the neck hand and the lap sau hand at the same time.

Left Bong sau

Using the sideling stance you can easily drop the hand that is currently located around the back of the neck to bong sau on the inside of the dummy's left arm- it's on your right.

Tan da

Maintaining contact with your bong sau, and stepping to the right side your bong sau hand should roll nicely into tan sau, circle your left leg behind the dummy's leg on the side you are standing and dai cheung your right hand into the dummy's area between the two up arms and the lower arms, but make all these move in one action- this is how the power is released.

High Jum/low gaan

Rotating your leg out from behind the dummy's leg and place it down into a 45 degree sideling stance facing left as you do so use the right hand that's is currently in dai cheung to form a jum sau on the outside of the left dummy arm, at the same time your hand that is in tan sau to gaan sau and makes contact with the lower single arm.

The Wooden Dummy – Our Forgiving Friend

Kwun sau

With a half step, move to the left and switch hands so that the gaan sau on the lower single arm comes up and hits the inside of the dummy's right arm and the hand currently in a high jum sau should drop down and make contact with the left side of the lower single arm, this should all happen simultaneously- this action is called kwun sau which means rotating hands.

Disconnected Tan da

Disconnecting your arms from the dummy step left a little further than you did when you went to the right, having your right man sau up and your left wu sau launch forward locking out the dummy leg with your right leg, block the dummy right arm on the outside using tan sau and hit the dummy chest area with dai cheung, and again this should all happen simultaneously.

High Jum/low gaan

Rotating your leg out from behind the dummy's leg and place it down into a 45 degree sideling stance facing right as you do so use the left hand that's is currently in dai cheung to form a jum sau on the outside of the right dummy arm, at the same time your hand that is in tan sau to gaan sau and makes contact with the lower single arm.

The Wooden Dummy – Our Forgiving Friend

Right high jum/left heun sau

Coming to the end of the first part of the form circle your left hand over the dummy's right arm so you hand end up blocking the inside of that arm, then bringing your arm that is currently in gaan sau in a slight curve to the outside of the dummy's left arm into an upper pointing jum sau so you should be looking at the palm of the right hand with fingers pointing upwards

Right lap sau / left dai cheung

Take your right hand currently in jum sau and grab that arm you are currently connected to and hit the dummy with palm up of the left hand slamming it into the dummy's chest area.

and finish in bai chong ready for the next section unless you'd like to finish with a double jum sau and a double tok sau.

Section Two - Form - Performed once

Right Pak Sau

As you have reset to the bai chong position, change guard and using your right palm hit the inside of the dummy's right arm.

Left Pak Sau

From that position change guard and hit the inside of the dummy's left arm with a pak sau from your left hand.

The Wooden Dummy – Our Forgiving friend

Right Pak Sau

Again change guard and using your right palm hit the inside of the dummy's right arm completing three pak sau's

Pressing Pak Sau

This left pak sau is angled downward and draws towards you like you are polishing the top of the arm.

Shat Geng Sau

Now keeping the left palm down, shoot forward and enact a throat strike with the left hand.

Dai Kuen

Withdrawing the striking left hand back but keeping it as a cover, punch with the currently free right hand to the stomach; this is the only punch you will see in the dummy form.

Pak Sau

This is now repeated on the other side so you see the right hand pak sau angled downward and drawn towards you like you are polishing the top of the arm.

Shat Geng Sau

Keeping the right palm down shoot forward and enact a throat strike

Dai Kuen

Withdrawing the striking hand back but keeping it as a cover, strike with the currently free left hand to the stomach.

Section Two - Form - Side One

Right dai bong sau

With your left hand in wu sau sink your stance and make contact with the lower single arm with a low bong sau.

Right fak da

After the dai bong sau is performed hit under the dummy's right arm with a fak sau while placing a pak sau to the outside of the dummy's right arm, thus checking the hand.

Right Wang Gerk

After this step backwards at a 45 degree angle just enough to put you in kicking range of the dummy's body then drive a side kick into the dummy.

Section Two - Form - Side Two

Left dai bong sau

After the kick, move right across the centre of the dummy positioned to perform a dai bong sau with your left arm on the single lower arm and just enough to move in for the fak da.

Left fak da

If you move to the correct position you should be able to do a dai bong sau and then perform the fak da from that position, remember the fak sau strikes under the left arm of the dummy and the right hand is in pak sau checking the left arm of the dummy.

Left Wang Gerk

Move out backwards from your current position and at a 45 degree angle just far enough to perform a clear crisp kick with power without feeling cramped but not so far that you can't kick properly.

High Jum/low gaan

Rotating your leg out from behind the dummy's leg and place it down into a 45 degree sideling stance facing left as you do so use the right hand that is currently in dai cheung to form a jum sau on the outside of the left dummy arm, at the same time your hand that is in tan sau to gaan sau and makes contact with the lower single arm.

Left high jum/right heun sau

Coming to the end of the first part of the form circle you right hand over the dummies left arm so you hand end up blocking the inside of that arm, then bringing your arm that is currently in gaan sau in a slight curve to the outside of the dummies right arm into an upper pointing jum sau so you should be looking at the palm of the left hand with fingers poiting upwards

Left lap sau / right jing cheung

Take your left hand currently in jum sau and grab that arm you are currently connected to and hit the dummy with palm up of the right hand slamming it into the dummies face area. and finish in bai chong ready for the next section unless you like to finish with a double jum sau and a double tok sau.

Left high jum/right heun sau

Coming to the end of the first part of the form circle your right hand over the dummy's left arm so your hand ends up blocking the inside of that arm, then bringing your arm that is currently in gaan sau in a slight curve to the outside of the dummy's right arm into an upper pointing jum sau so you should be looking at the palm of the left hand with fingers pointing upwards

Left lap sau / right jing cheung

Take your left hand currently in jum sau and grab that arm you are currently connected to and hit the dummy with palm up of the right hand slamming it into the dummy's face area. and finish in bai chong ready for the next section unless you'd like to finish with a double jum sau and a double tok sau.

Section Three - Form - Performed Once

Sheung Jum Sau

Start with both arms pressing against the outside of each dummy arm, your left against the outside of the right upper arm and your right against the outside of the dummy's left upper arm.

Sheung Huen Sau

At the same time start to travel from the outside, maintaining a stick to the arms, then over to the inside of each arms using huen sau.

Sheung Dai cheung

Once your arms are no longer obstructed by the upper arms of the dummy, drop your knees and enact a strike to the bellow of the dummy.

Sheung Tan Sau

Quickly return to tan sau using both hands, the tan sau's should be on the inside or the upper dummy arms. Just stay there a split second.

Sheung Juk Cheung

Using each hand strike each side of the dummy's neck area as quickly as possible after leaving the prior tan sau's

Sheung Jum Sau

Finish with both arms pressing against the outside of each dummy arm, your left against the outside of the right upper arm and your right against the outside of the dummy's left upper arm.

Section Three - Form - Side One

Right Jum / Left Heun Sau

Circle inwards over the right dummy arms with your left hand using huen sau and combining that with the 45 degree step from right to left and stop on the inside of the dummy's arm.

Left Jum / Right Heun Sau

Then start to change the 45 step to the other direction as you circle the right hand over the top of the dummy's left hand and stop on the inside, at the same time the left hand that is currently in an inside huen sau, let it drop under the same dummy arm and travel to the outside into a jum sau fingers pointing up.

Right Jum / Left Heun Sau

Again start change the 45 degrees step to the other direction as you circle the left hand over the top of the dummy's left hand and stop on the inside, at the same time the left hand that is currently in an inside huen sau, let it drop under the same dummy arm and travel to the outside into a jum sau fingers pointing up.

Left Lap Sau / Right Jing Cheung

Go to a front stance facing the dummy again and then grab the dummy's right arm with your left hand and then from where you right jum sau is positioned, drive that in to the body of the dummy above the upper arms with your fingers pointing to the ceiling.

Right Bong Sau

Now with the hand that struck the dummy, perform a bong sau to the inside of the dummy's right arm at the same time bring the left hand to wu sau and performing the 45 degree step going right to left.

Tan Da With Low Front Kick - (Dai Dung Gerk)

Maintaining contact with your bong sau, and stepping to the left side, your bong sau hand should roll nicely into tan sau, hit with dai cheung using your left hand into the dummy's area between the two up arms and the lower arms, but make all these move in one continuous flowing action. The final step is to kick in to the knee of the dummy with your heel on the right leg.

Section Three - Form - Side Two

High Jum/low gaan

As you are currently in a 45 degree sideling stance facing right, use the left hand that's is currently in dai cheung to form a jum sau on the outside of the right dummy arm, at the same time your hand that is in tan sau to gaan sau and makes contact with the lower single arm.

Left Jum / Right Heun Sau

Circle inwards over the left dummy arms with your right hand using huen sau and combining that with the 45 step from left to right and stop on the inside of the dummy's arm.

Right Jum / Left Heun Sau

Then start to change the 45 step to the other direction as you circle the left hand over the top of the dummy's right hand and stop on the inside, at the same time the right hand that is currently in an inside huen sau, let it drop under the same dummy arm and travel to the outside into a jum sau fingers pointing up.

Left Jum / Right Heun Sau

Again start change the 45 degree step to the other direction as you circle the right hand over the top of the dummy's right hand and stop on the inside, at the same time the right hand that is currently in an inside huen sau, let it drop under the same dummy arm and travel to the outside into a jum sau fingers pointing up.

Right Lap Sau / Left Jing Cheung

Go to a front stance facing the dummy again and then grab the dummy's left arm with your right hand and then from where you left jum sau is positioned, drive that in to the body of the dummy above the upper arms with your fingers pointing to the ceiling.

Left Bong Sau

Now with the hand that struck the dummy, perform a bong sau to the inside of the dummy's left arm at the same time bring the right hand to wu sau and performing the 45 step going left to right.

Tan Da With Low Front Kick - (Dai Dung Gerk)

Maintaining contact with your bong sau, and stepping to the right side, your bong sau hand should roll nicely into tan sau, hit with dai cheung using your right hand into the dummy's area between the two up arms and the lower arms, but make all these move in one action. The final step is to kick in to the knee of the dummy with your heel on the left leg.

High Jum/low gaan

Rotating your leg out from behind the dummy's leg and place it down into a 45 degree sideling stance facing left as you do so use the right hand that's is currently in dai cheung to form a jum sau on the outside of the left dummy arm, at the same time your hand that is in tan sau to gaan sau and makes contact with the lower single arm.

The Wooden Dummy – Our Forgiving friend

Left high jum/right heun sau

Coming to the end of the first part of the form circle your right hand over the dummy's left arm so your hand ends up blocking the inside of that arm, then bringing your arm that is currently in gaan sau in a slight curve to the outside of the dummy's right arm into an upper pointing jum sau so you should be looking at the palm of the left hand with fingers pointing upwards

Left lap sau / right jing cheung

Take your left hand currently in jum sau and grab that arm you are currently connected to and hit the dummy with palm up of the right hand slamming it into the dummy's face area. and finish in bai chong ready for the next section unless you'd like to finish with a double jum sau and a double tok sau.

Section Four - Po Pie Chueng

This section is all about using po pie and contains four different ways to use it. Both hands are used and *when the hands are in the double palm strike position the wrists should be kept close to each other.*

Section Four - Form - Performed Once

Right man Sau

From your guard position make contact using your right arm with the inside of right arm of the dummy.

Left Jut sau

From your continued guard position, lift your right wrist and make contact with the inside of the dummy's left arm.

Right Jum Sau

Turning the body 45 degrees from the right to left perform a jum sau on the inside of the dummy's right arm keeping your rear hand in wu sau.

Cow sau

Following the jum sau switch your stance 45 degrees from the left to the right, while doing allow the jum sau hand to maintain contact but rock over the top of the dummy's right hand using huen sau, the wu sau hand should come forward and strike the right side of the dummy's body with dai cheung.

Section Four - Form - Application One

Kwun Sau

Maintaining the position of the feet, the left hand in dai cheung should simultaneously make contact with the lower dummy arm in dai bong sau while the hand currently in cow sau, leading with the elbow dropping between the upper dummy arms, travelling to the inside of the dummies left arm ending up in tan sau, thus creating the kwun sau (rotating hand) in the what is recognised as kwun sau.

Po Pie - Centre Strike

From the Kwun Sau position centre off your stance again until you are in Siu Lim Tau and facing the dummy and keeping the hands along their current horizontal plains, turn both hands with the palms facing toward the dummy's body in the centre, keeping one hand below the two upper arms with the fingers pointing to the ground and the other above with the fingers pointing to the ceiling, then driving your push both hands into the dummy.

Section Four - Form - Left Side Strike

Left Bong Sau

After the strike, turn you body 45 degrees from left to right and using your lower left hand, allow that to rise forming a bong sau to the inside of the dummy's right arm- at the same time bring your right hand up into wu sau

Po Pie

Maintaining contact with the hand that is in bong sau, transition still making contact under the dummy's right arm, and stepping to your right side, still maintaining contact, when you reach the outside switch the bong sau hand in to the upper palm strike position with the fingers pointing to the ceiling and now bring your right hand currently in wu sau forward to make the lower palm strike hand with the fingers pointing down to the ground, circle the left leg around the dummy's leg and then thrust both hands into the dummy.

Section Four - Form - Back to Centre

Jum Sau / Gann sau

Bringing the left leg back from where it came in the last move, move your left hand to gaan sau on the lower arm and your

The Wooden Dummy – Our Forgiving Friend

right arm in to jum sau, centre off to the dummy again and put your left hand in the lower position in to a palm strike with the fingers pointing down and the right hand in to a palm strike with fingers pointing up and drive forward with both hand in to the dummy.

Po Pie

position and keeping the hands along their current horizontal plains, turn both hands with the palms facing toward the dummy's body in the centre, keeping one hand below the two upper arms with the fingers pointing to the ground and the other above with the fingers point to the ceiling, push both hands into the dummy.

Section Four - Form - Right Side Strike

Right Bong Sau

While transitioning your right arm into bong sau making contact with the inside of the dummy's right arm change your stance to 45 degrees moving right to left, bring your left hand into wu sau.

Po Pie

In this final version of the po pie, you need to disconnect from the dummy and then drive in from the outside and which is 45 degrees, so stepping out to the left side, bring your left hand up in to a palm with the fingers pointing to the ceiling and the right hand in to the lower palm and while using your forward biu ma drive in to the side of the dummy.

High Jum/low gaan

Rotating your leg out from behind the dummy's leg and place it down into a 45 degree sideling stance facing right as you do so use the left hand that's is currently in dai cheung to form a jum sau on the outside of the right dummy arm, at the same time your hand that is in tan sau to gaan sau and makes contact with the lower single arm.

Right high jum/left heun sau

Coming to the end of the first part of the form circle you left hand over the dummy's right arm so your hand ends up blocking the inside of that arm, then bringing your arm that is currently in gaan sau in a slight curve to the outside of the dummy's left arm into an upper pointing jum sau so you should be looking at the palm of the right hand with fingers pointing upwards

Right lap sau / left dai cheung

Take your right hand currently in jum sau and grab that arm you are currently connected to and hit the dummy with palm up of the left hand slamming it into the dummy's chest area. and finish in bai chong ready for the next section unless you like to finish with a double jum sau and a double tok sau.

Section Five - Form

Right side - Jum sau / gann sau

Nothing exciting here, turn your body right to left through 45 degrees and perform a right jum sau and a left gaan sau.

Left side - Jum sau /gann sau

Switch your stance the other direction travelling through 90 degrees and change your arms so that the left is the jum sau and the right is the gaan sau.

The Fan sau

The following technique is known as the fan sau and the section is referred to as the fan sau section.

Left Bong, lap, shat geng sau, juk cheung - (lap da)

From the right gaan sau, move your arm right, and out and over the top of the dummy's left arm arriving in a bong sau on the inside or the dummy's right hand that immediately turns into a lap sau, the free left hand hits the neck of the dummy using the knife part of the hand, once the strike has happened withdraw that hand and grab the dummy's arm on the same side as the strike, releasing the other hand to again it the neck using juk cheung.

Right Bong, lap, shat geng sau, juk cheung - (lap da)

After hitting with the right hand withdraw it to wu sau and release the hand and travel over to and under the dummy's left arm in a bong sau that immediately turns into a lap sau, the free right hand hits the neck of the dummy using the knife part of the hand, once the strike has happened withdraw that hand and grab the dummy's arm on the same side as the strike, releasing the other hand to again hit the neck using juk cheung.

Right Bong Sau to Tan Da

The left hand goes to wu sau and your right arm travels in bong sau over to the inside of right dummy arm on arrival step sideways and into tan da striking the dummy with dai cheung to the torso.

Right Tep Sun Gerk

Finally, with the leg furthest away from the dummy (the left leg) kick the side of the dummy, Funny story nobody actually knows the name of this kick so I did some research and the closest I could get was "no shadow kick", why? If the kick comes at you from the front you cannot see it and so it is called shadow kick, but If you perform the kick from the side you can see it coming hence the name "no shadow kick"

Left Bong Sau to Tan da

While stepping from the left to right transition your left arm over the top of the dummy's right arms and arrive in bong sau on the inside of the dummy's left arm, step sideways again and into tan da striking the dummy with dai cheung to the torso.

Left Tep Sun Gerk

This time kick with your right leg which is the furthest away from the dummy.

High Jum/low gaan

Rotating your leg out from behind the dummy's leg and place it down into a 45 degree sideling stance facing left as you do so use the right hand that's is currently in dai cheung to form a jum sau on the outside of the left dummy arm, at the same time your hand that is in tan sau to gaan sau and makes contact with the lower single arm.

The Wooden Dummy – Our Forgiving Friend

Left high jum/right heun sau

Coming to the end of the first part of the form circle you right hand over the dummy's left arm so you hand end up blocking the inside of that arm, then bringing your arm that is currently in gaan sau in a slight curve to the outside of the dummy's right arm into an upper pointing jum sau so you should be looking at the palm of the left hand with fingers pointing upwards

Left lap sau / right jing cheung

Take your left hand currently in jum sau and grab that arm you are currently connected to and hit the dummy with palm up of the right hand slamming it into the dummy's face area. and finish in bai chong ready for the next section unless you'd like to finish with a double jum sau and a double tok sau.

Section Six - Form

Left Tan Sau and right Jing sun gerk

In the opening of section six we first take a small central step backwards and then make a bridge point using an inside tan sau, on the dummy's upper right arm, we then drive the right foot forward, kicking with the heel in to the dummy.

The Wooden Dummy – Our Forgiving friend

Right Bong sau and right chai gerk

Keeping the right foot air bound, twist the left foot changing the angle of your body right to left, at the same time bringing your right hand to bong sau and the left hand in to wu sau, next drive the outside of the foot, using the heel and not the blade of the foot, drive it in to the leg of the dummy.

Right Tan Sau and left jing sun jerk

Again, take a small central step backwards and then make a bridge point using an inside tan sau, on the dummy's upper left arm, we then drive the left foot forward, kicking with the heel in to the dummy.

Left bong sau and left chai gerk

With the left foot air bound, twist the right foot changing the angle of your body left to right, at the same time bringing your left hand to bong sau and the right hand in to wu sau, next drive the outside of the foot, using the heel and not the blade of the foot, drive it in to the leg of the dummy.

The Wooden Dummy – Our Forgiving friend

Right Gum sau

After returning to siu lim tau ma, switch your stance to 45 degrees and drive you hand in to the lower dummy arm, pressing down and to the left at a 45 degree angle.

Left side pak da

Circle the right leg around the dummy's leg and drive your right hand using a palm into the space between the upper and lower arms and cover with your pak sau.

Left Gum Sau

Bring the right foot back to where it started and sink the weight on the left foot and this time drive your left hand down and across at 45 degrees.

Right pak da

This time circle the left foot around the dummy's leg and drive your left hand into the dummy making sure to cover with pak sau.

High Jum/low gaan

Rotating your leg out from behind the dummy's leg and place it down into a 45 degree sideling stance facing left as you do so use the right hand that's is currently in dai cheung to form a jum sau on the outside of the left dummy arm, at the same time your hand that is in tan sau to gaan sau and makes contact with the lower single arm.

High Jum/low gaan

Rotating your leg out from behind the dummy's leg and place it down into a 45 degree sideling stance facing left as you do so use the right hand that's is currently in dai cheung to form a jum sau on the outside of the left dummy arm, at the same time your hand that is in tan sau to gaan sau and makes contact with the lower single arm.

Left high jum/right heun sau

Circle your right hand over the dummy's left arm so that your hand ends up blocking the inside of that arm, then bringing your arm that is currently in gaan sau in a slight curve to the outside of the dummy's right arm into an upper pointing jum sau so you should be looking at the palm of the left hand with fingers pointing upwards.

Left lap sau / right jing cheung

Take your left hand currently in jum sau and grab that arm you are currently connected to and hit the dummy with palm up of the right hand slamming it into the dummy's face area. and finish in bai chong ready for the next section unless you'd like to finish with a double jum sau and a double tok sau.

Section Seven - Form

Right dai bong sau

There are three levels of bong sau, the first is the standard one that meets the normal arm height. The next bong sau covers the middle gates this is called dai bong sau, and there is one that covers the lower gates and this is called haar lo bong sau, the one here is blocking a gut punch and is called dai bong sau.

Move the body to a 45 degree side stance from right to left and make contact with the lower dummy arm using your dai bong sau by rolling it in to the lower arm.

Left dai bong sau

Move your body through 90 degrees from left to right and again roll your bong sau in to the lower dummy arm.

Right dai bong sau

Move your body through 90 degrees from right to left and again roll your bong sau in to the lower dummy arm.

Right tan sau

After the right dai bong sau, bring the right hand up into tan sau on the inside of the dummy's left hand.

Right Juk cheung

Immediately after that using the hand in tan sau strike the upper gate area of the dummy with juk cheung.

Left side pak sau with dai dung gerk

After the right juk cheung, side step to the left to the outside gate of the dummy and turn in to a 45 degree stance from left to right and perform a pak sau against the out side of the dummy's right arm once contact has been made kick into the knee section of the dummy's leg.

Left dai bong sau

Move back to the centre of the dummy keeping the body at a 45 degree side stance from left to right and make contact with the lower dummy arm using your dai bong sau by rolling it in to the lower arm.

Right dai bong sau

Move your body through 90 degrees from right to left and again roll your bong sau in to the lower dummy arm.

Left dai bong sau

Move your body through 90 degrees from left to right and

again roll your bong sau in to the lower dummy arm.

Left tan sau

After the left dai bong sau, bring the left hand up into tan sau on the inside of the dummy's right hand.

Left Juk cheung

Immediately after that using the hand in tan sau strike the upper gate are of the dummy with juk cheung.

Right side pak sau with dai dung gerk

After the left juk cheung, side step to the right to the outside gate of the dummy and turn in to a 45 degree stance from right to left and perform a pak sau against the out side of the dummy's left arm- once contact has been made kick into the knee section of the dummy's leg.

Right bong sau

Then side step from right to left and allow the right hand currently in pak sau travel over the top of the arms and into an inside bong sau making contact with inside of the dummy's right arm

Left side -sheung lap sau with soo gerk

Immediately transition in to a lap sau and bringing the other hand under the arms you have grabbed so that one hand is grabbing on the top and the other hand is grabbing underneath, then drive your right heel in to the dummy's leg

The Wooden Dummy – Our Forgiving Friend

Left bong sau

Stepping from left to right allow the left hand travel over the top of the arms and into an inside bong sau making contact with inside of the dummy's left arm

The Wooden Dummy – Our Forgiving friend

Right side -sheung lap sau with soo gerk

Immediately transition in to a lap sau and bringing the other hand under the arms you have grabbed so that one hand is grabbing on the top and the other hand is grabbing underneath, then drive your left heel in to the dummy's leg

High Jum/low gaan

Rotating your leg out from behind the dummy's leg and place it down into a 45 degree sideling stance facing left as you do so use the right hand that's is currently in dai cheung to form a jum sau on the outside of the left dummy arm, at the same time your hand that is in tan sau to gaan sau and makes contact with the lower single arm.

Left high jum/right heun sau

Coming to the end of the first part of the form circle your right hand over the dummy's left arm so your hand ends up blocking the inside of that arm, then bringing your arm that is currently in gaan sau in a slight curve to the outside of the dummy's right arm into an upper pointing jum sau so you should be looking at the palm of the left hand with fingers pointing upwards.

Left lap sau / right jing cheung

Take your left hand currently in jum sau and grab that arm you are currently connected to and hit the dummy with the palm up of the right hand slamming it into the dummy's face area. and finish in bai chong ready for the next section unless you like to finish with a double jum sau and a double tok sau.

And that completes the form.

Dummy Application

Pak sau

With pak sau as seen in section two of the dummy form, some assume that you are doing pak sau on the inside of the arms, the arms should be thought of as being crossed here, if they were not crossed, it would not be repeated, and here is why, when using an inside pak sau, one hand would pak and the other hand would hit as quickly as possible as the attacker can response with their free hand, thus explaining why this is meant to be used on the outside to fold the arms in as seen below.

Pak sau to stomach punch

For those that do not know, pak sau san be pressed or pushed to the side or pressed down or pushed down to the ground, it's the action itself that gives it the name pak sau, in this instance the attacker threw out right fist and in doing so I dispersed it across my body, I then through forward a shat geng sau aiming for the throat, but it was blocked, so I returned to the pak sau and hit him in the stomach.

Fak da

This technique can be used against the throat area, in this case however I went low, taking my head out of range of his fist and because I was in a low position I was able to strike under the armpit covering with pak sau so he could not swing his arm back to hit me.

Fak da to wan gerk

In the previous scenario I was fighting multiple attackers so I would hit once and move on however if I am faced with just one attacker I can continue with a second strike, as I with draw I bring my bong sau and wu sau up to protect my withdrawal but remaining in kick distance and striking with the heel, this is a side kick and is called wan gerk.

Sheung dai cheung

The application here can be performed with one arm if the grabber is only using one arm or two and has performed in the dummy form, if you have been grabbed by both arms, in the pictures you can see that my arms using jum sau push the opponents arms inward, when doing this, the natural response is to press back so the attacker tries to maintain the gap between their arms, this makes it easy to circle each hand inward using huen sau and pushing outward to make space to attack VERY QUICKLY with both hand to the low ribs, if you travel too slowly they can recover and hit you.

Sheung juk cheung

As I just mentioned if you do not move quickly they will recover, if you see them attempting to recover, then you should bring you hand up in to two tan sau's to stop them, again very quickly
Strike to the neck area this a neck palm strike in Cantonese called juk cheung, this would not be performed ever with one

hand as you are on the centre and you can be hit by the free hand.

Applying jum da

In the third part of the form you see circle hand performed three times one way and then three times the other, the application for this can be best described from the double grab, my right hand that cannot be seen in the picture be below comes up and hooks the inside of his left arm using huen sau, my other hand jams in to his forearm with my forearm with jum sau, while checking that arm, the huen sau slides forward on the inside of the other arm as to maintain some kind of blocking and strikes the chest.

The Wooden Dummy – Our Forgiving friend

Bong sau to pak da with kick (disconnected)

At the end of section three we are on the centre, however to get to the outside gate area, I cover with a bong sau while stepping out with wan gerk, once the outside his reach I turn back in to the 45 degree stance, I then transition the bong arm to a covering tan sau and strike the rib cage, then finally follow up with kick (dai dung gerk)

Po pie cheung (connected)

This brings us to the application in section four of the form, this part is commonly known and the po pie section, po pie is made up of a palm with fingers pointing the ceiling and a palm mirroring it with the wrists as close as possible to each other with the fingers pointing downward.

In this application of po pie, I received a punch from the right hand and used pak sau to control it, this forced the attacker to use the left arm which I then used bong sau to get to his left side where I pin the arm, I then form my po pie and drive forward with the strike with a slight incline upwards.

Po pie cheung (disconnected)

In the first application of po pie I used the left arm of the attacker to advance on him, this time, I am just going to get my head out of the way. Step quickly with wan ma to get to the outside, then form my po pie with left arm at the top just like in the form again drive forward and slight upward to make my attacker travel away from me.

The Wooden Dummy – Our Forgiving Friend

Jum Sau / Gaan Sau

This brings us to section five commonly know as the fan sau section, but before this we see to jum sau / gaan sau's one on each side, some schools of thought will use this against a forward coming kick, if you have ever received a kick from a skilled karateka, you would not try to take on such a kick, in Wing Chun we commonly use hands for hands and feet for feet, in the pictures below imagine that the first strike coming in was very strong, so I blocked it with jum sau and covered it with gaan sau, as a result the attacker hit with the other hand with the same power and I covered it again, finally I pinned it down with pak sau and hit with my free hand.

Fan Da

In chi sau we use a set of movements that are recognised as fan sau, when chi sau techniques are performed but not from chi sau (wrists sticking) we move to the realm of fighting application and this is called gor sau, so with that in mind below you see me disperse a strike from the right hand and push the hand down the invite the other hand to come forward, and as it does so I transition to bong sau leading to lap sau and hit with my free right hand, I then bring the right hand to lap sau and hit with my left hand, this would continue till the fight is one by getting faster and faster each time.

Tep Sun Gerk

The 'no shadow kick' is the translation of Cantonese meaning a kick that can be seen coming hence the name, in this example of the application from section five the attacker throws a forward punch of the right hand and I block it with downward pak sau, inviting him to hit with the other hand by pushing his right hand down I respond with the same arm and cover with bong sau, at the same time I am stepping sideways with wan ma from where is transition to tan sau and kick with tep sun gerk.

Jing gerk to Chai gerk

Bringing us to section six and the opening kick combo, it's the first time in Wing Chun where you actually ever use a kick combination so the lesson is important and should be given some thought why that is, my answer to this was that it exists to develop the ability to balance on one leg and kick a multiple of times without placing the kicking foot down. In the slides below you can see the attacker advance on me but is out of range and entering quickly, so I threw my front kick out to meet his arrival which forced him to stop advancing on me leaving his forward leg exposed, from here is turned to a side kick know hear as chai gerk and drove that into his shin just below the knee.

Pak Da

The second part of section six the attacker comes forward again with right strike and bringing his right left forward for power, I then circle around the lead leg, pinning his striking right arm with pak sau and hitting the low rib cage with a dai cheung.

Dai bong sau to juk cheung

As we move through the sections of the form and we arrive here at the seventh and last section we open with dai bong sau, again with a right hand attack coming towards me this time to the stomach area, I sweep across to bridge this with bong sau and as I do he throws his left hand at me so I respond with a tan sau and quickly use juk cheung to hit him in the face.

The Wooden Dummy – Our Forgiving friend

Pak to dai dung gerk

Below we see the attacker coming forward again with a right strike, its coming quite quickly so I don't want to be there when it arrives so I use the side step to get out of the way, turn in to my 45 stance and pin his right arm with a left pak sau, to finish him off, I drive my foot in to his knee with dai dung gerk.

The Wooden Dummy – Our Forgiving friend

Double lap to soo gerk

In the final application in the dummy form, oddly enough I am attacked with a right strike which I block with pak sau, this time I don't invite him to ht me with his left hand so he hits high and I cross his centreline using bong sau automatically transitioning to lap sau, while positioning my foot into his lower shin area while pulling his left arm, and because he can't move his foot he goes flying, think of it as tripping someone, however if you don't like them you can really jam your heel with a swing into his lower shin, that is really going to hurt, then wave goodbye.

The Wooden Dummy – Our Forgiving Friend

The Wooden Dummy – Our Forgiving friend

This concludes the application of the dummy form, there are a few other techniques in there too, just remember to stay true to the concepts of Wing Chun and how things work as a rule of thumb and you will keep it real.

Common types of dummy

There have been many versions of the wooden dummy made over the years to suit everyone budget, but a as rule you can expect to pay a lot of cash for a good dummy, below you will see dummies the go in to the ground standard wall mount and even corner framed dummies, they should be made or wood but you can also make them from plastic too.

The Wooden Dummy – Our Forgiving friend

The Wooden Dummy – Our Forgiving Friend

The Full form

Section One

The Wooden Dummy – Our Forgiving Friend

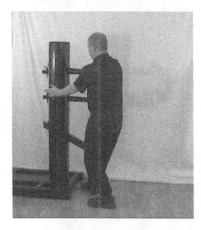

The Wooden Dummy – Our Forgiving friend

The Wooden Dummy – Our Forgiving Friend

The Wooden Dummy – Our Forgiving friend

The Wooden Dummy – Our Forgiving Friend

Section Two

The Wooden Dummy – Our Forgiving Friend

The Wooden Dummy – Our Forgiving friend

The Wooden Dummy – Our Forgiving Friend

Section Three

The Wooden Dummy – Our Forgiving Friend

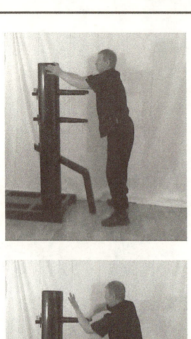

The Wooden Dummy – Our Forgiving friend

The Wooden Dummy – Our Forgiving Friend

The Wooden Dummy – Our Forgiving friend

Section Four

The Wooden Dummy – Our Forgiving friend

The Wooden Dummy – Our Forgiving Friend

The Wooden Dummy – Our Forgiving friend

Section Five

The Wooden Dummy – Our Forgiving friend

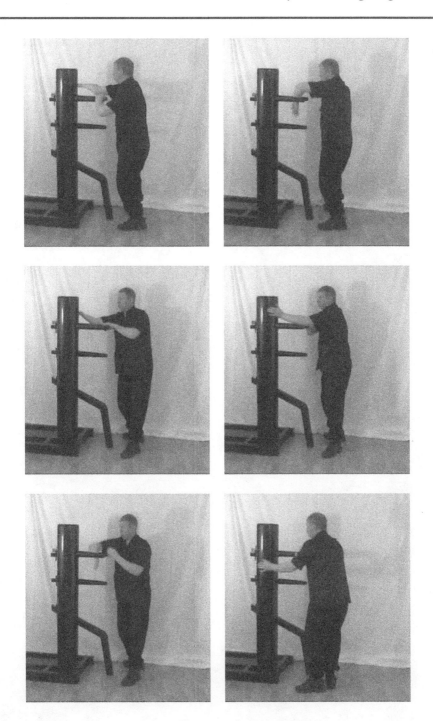

The Wooden Dummy – Our Forgiving Friend

The Wooden Dummy – Our Forgiving friend

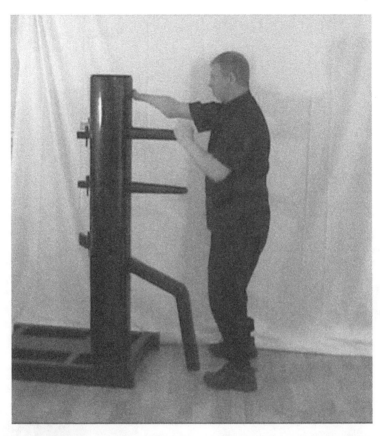

Section Six

The Wooden Dummy – Our Forgiving friend

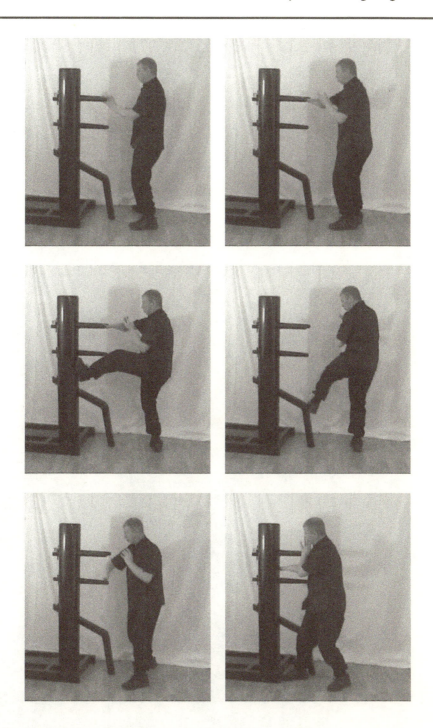

The Wooden Dummy – Our Forgiving Friend

The Wooden Dummy – Our Forgiving friend

The Wooden Dummy – Our Forgiving Friend

Section Seven

The Wooden Dummy – Our Forgiving friend

The Wooden Dummy – Our Forgiving Friend

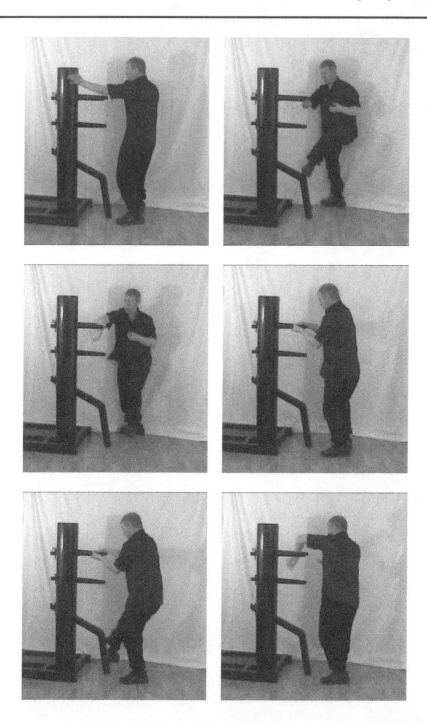

The Wooden Dummy – Our Forgiving friend

Thanks

A huge thanks for the assistance of my local students for their help filming the application sequences for the book, and to everyone else who assisted me in the completion of this book.

And a big thanks to you for purchasing this book and I hope you find it helpful with your training.

If at anytime I can help you with your training, you can contact me at

Website: http://www.wingchun-ipman.com

email: mark_beardsell@yahoo.co.uk

Facebook: https://www.facebook.com/mbeardsell

Twitter: https://twitter.com/mbeardsell

CPSIA information can be obtained
at www.ICGtesting.com
Printed in the USA
FSHW010948110520
70121FS